The Stories of Juana Briones

Alta California Pioneer

By Glenda Richter

Illustrations by Della Heywood

Bookhandler Press
Bonita, California

Editor: Nancy Lemke
Designer: Andrea Miles

ISBN 0-9700379-0-2 Hardcover
ISBN 0-9700379-1-0 Softcover

Bookhandler Press
3597 Lomacitas Lane
Bonita, California 91902
www.bookhandler.com

Library of Congress Cataloging-in-Publication Data

Richter, Glenda.
    The stories of Juana Briones : Alta California pioneer / by Glenda
Richter ; illustrated by Della Heywood.
        p. cm.
    Summary: Presents the life of a woman whose family members were
among the first Hispanic settlers to come to California to establish ranch-
es and to help build missions.

    1. Briones, Juana, 1802–1889–Juvenile literature. 2. Women pioneers–
California–Biography–Juvenile literature. 3. Hispanic American women–
California–Biography–Juvenile literature.
4. Pioneers–California–Biography–Juvenile literature. 5. Frontier and
pioneer life–California–Juvenile literature. 6. California–History–19th
century–Juvenile literature. 7. California–Biography–Juvenile literature.
[1. Briones, Juana, 1802–1889. 2. Frontier and pioneer life–West (U.S.) 3.
California–History. 4. Women–Biography.] I. Heywood, Della, ill. II.
Title.
    F864.B76 R53 2002
    979.4'04'092–dc21

                                                                    2001005828

2

The Stories of Juana Briones

Text Note:

Boldfaced words are vocabulary words. Their definitions are in the glossary.

Italicized words are Spanish words not commonly used in English.

Dear Readers,

A few months ago, I came to know a remarkable woman. Her name is Juana Briones. She was a California pioneer who was a citizen of Spain, Mexico, and the United States, all without traveling more than a few miles from where she was born!

Her mother came all the way from Mexico on horseback with Juan Bautista de Anza in 1775, and Juana was born in 1802 in Villa de Branciforte, a **pueblo** near Santa Cruz, California. When she was a young bride, she moved to the San Francisco Presidio and then later to Yerba Buena, the pueblo that became the city of San Francisco. She was actually the third resident of San Francisco!

As I learned about Juana, I was amazed that she accomplished so much and was so well known and admired during her lifetime. Back then, women didn't have many opportunities to do things on their own. She must have been very unusual, I thought. And she was. She cared for so many sick people that one newspaper called her California's Clara Barton. Clara Barton was a famous nurse who began the Red Cross. Juana was skilled with herbs to treat illnesses, and she set broken bones and delivered babies.

She also helped sailors escape from the hard life of a mariner in the 1800s. In those days, men were highjacked against their will to work on ships. They were forced to sail

all over the world, and many died from starvation and disease. It was a terrible life. Juana dared to help the sailors by hiding them in her house until they could escape.

One of the most remarkable things about Juana Briones was that she was a landowner. This may not seem unusual today, but it was almost unheard of in the early years of California for married women to own property in their own name. Juana even held on to her land when California became part of the United States. Many Hispanic landowners lost their land to Americans. Juana fought all the way to the United States Supreme Court to prove her land was hers, and she won.

You might ask how I learned all this about Juana. That would be a very good question. I read articles from the International Women's Museum, an organization that sponsored a plaque to honor Juana in San Francisco. I read books about early California history and found information about her and her father, Marcos Briones, and her brothers, Gregorio and Felipe. I read books written by people who knew her and her family. Each bit of information was like a piece in a puzzle that fit together to make a picture of her life.

There were lots of things I could read, but one real problem I had was that Juana never learned to read or write, so I could not find anything she herself had written. But the more I read about her, and the more I read other people's memories of the times when she lived, the more I felt I knew her.

Then I began imagining how she lived. I imagined the stories her father and mother told her about their long journey to Alta California. I actually began to hear her words in my own head, telling the stories of her unusual and remarkable life!

Now I'd like to tell you these stories, as she might have told them to her own children and grandchildren. Perhaps, when you hear her stories, you will find her as surprising a woman as I did.

Glenda Richter
Jamul, California
2001

Dreams

For my sixtieth birthday in the summer of 1862 my family came home to Rancho La Purisima Concepción. The fiesta they planned was supposed to be a surprise for me, but in our family, secrets are hard to keep. I prepared for weeks. I cooked favorite dishes. I cleaned, and I made beds where there had never been beds before. Then, when my sisters and brothers, my children and grandchildren, my nieces and nephews began to arrive, I tried to act surprised and said, "Imagine! My family has come to see me!"

By the third day of dancing and singing and riding, everyone was tired, and the children begged for stories. We are a family that loves stories, and we have many to tell. This time, I wanted to tell the children the Briones family stories from beginning to end.

I called out, "Come, children. It's story time." They found places on blankets and stools in the shade of the **ramada,** and I began.

"First, I will tell you the stories Mama and Papa told me about coming to California, and then I will tell you about my life. Listen carefully, **mis hijos.** These stories tell you who you are."

My father, Marcos Briones, and my mother, Maria Isadora Tapia, could not read or write, but they were wonderful storytellers. And they taught us children who they were by telling us stories of their lives. When I was a girl, I loved Papa's adventure stories best—his stories of hunting grizzly bears and chasing wild Spanish horses. But as I grew, I realized that our family's stories were so closely connected to the beginnings of **Alta California** that they were nearly the same. The stories of our family were actually history!

Papa Marcos told my brothers and sisters—Gregorio, Felipe, Luz, Jachaca, Guadalupe—and me that these stories were a legacy to pass on to our children. He told us to remember each story just as he told it, and we promised, cross our hearts, that we would not forget a word.

Even though Papa was not a big man, his voice boomed through our house. Mama was usually quiet, tapping her foot to the rhythm of Papa's voice and sewing on something she was making to sell. But once she decided to tell her part of a story, her words flew out of her mouth.

My story and theirs begins long ago with the dreams of the king of Spain. The king, Papa told us, owned almost all of the Americas, but he dreamed of owning every inch of those continents! He sent explorers from New Spain up the

" Listen carefully, mis hijos. These stories tell you who you are."

Pacific Coast to claim everything they found for him. These explorers were dreamers too. Why else would they risk their lives going where no one had gone before? They dreamed of finding gold, and they traveled along miles and miles of coastline, claiming it all for the king. Unfortunately, they didn't find any gold, but they did find this new land called Alta California.

Many years later, in 1775, a new Spanish king worried that he might lose Alta California. Only about 70 Spaniards lived in California and hunters from Russia were moving in and claiming land too. To keep California for himself, the king decided to send Spanish settlers to populate the land. Fortunately for the king, a man named Juan Bautista de Anza had blazed a safe overland trail from **New Spain,** to Monterey in Alta California. The king chose this good man to lead a group of soldiers and settlers to their new home.

One day Captain Anza rode into Culiacán, New Spain where Mama was living with her parents. Mama was only a child then, and her Papa, Felipe Santiago Tapia, was a soldier in the Spanish Army. Grandpapa Tapia liked the looks of Captain Anza and the confident way he talked. The Captain asked some of the soldiers to join him and to bring their families to Alta California. He said the king needed them to build a presidio and a new mission on San Francisco Bay. The payment for the long journey over the 1,700-mile trail might be the chance to own land.

Right away Grandpapa said, "I am just the man for this adventure!" Then he went home to talk it over with his wife.

Now, Grandpapa was a restless man, who always wanted something new. He also had great faith that God would not provide an opportunity like this without providing the means to keep them safe. But his wife, my Grandmama Juana Maria Tapia, was not so sure California was a good idea. She was a practical woman, and she worried about life in a strange land. Could her children survive such a difficult journey? Would the Indians attack? Once they got there, would the corn grow? Would she find the herbs she needed for medicine? After much talk, Grandmama finally agreed with Grandpapa, and once they set their eyes north, they did not look back.

On September 27, 1775, Captain Anza led almost 200 people out of Tubac on the journey to San Francisco Bay, the site of the new mission. They looked like a moving village. There were many horses, mules, over 300 head of cattle, and enough supplies and ammunition to last them six months on the trail and the first six months in Alta California. There were exactly 165 mules. Grandpapa never forgot that number because he had to help unload them every night and load them again in the morning!

The king gave each person on the Anza expedition a fine Spanish horse to ride. Even the children rode or walked beside their horses. Although Mama was just a little girl, she was strong and could ride like the wind. Her Papa had to lift her into the saddle, but once she was there, she stayed all day, racing up and down the line of mules and riders.

For six months my grandparents, Mama, and the rest of the settlers rode and walked, sometimes afraid that they would not find water, sometimes afraid they would not find the trail. In all that time only one person died. She was a poor woman who gave birth to a baby only one day after

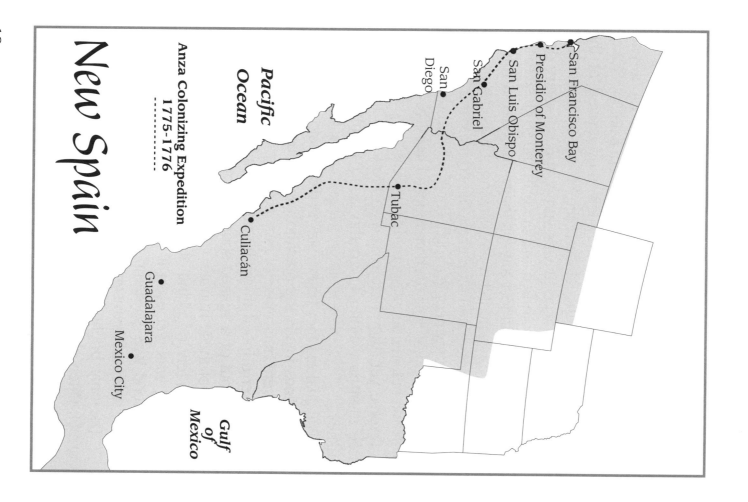

New Spain

Pacific
Ocean

Anza Colonizing Expedition
1775-1776
∙∙∙∙∙∙∙∙∙∙

San
Diego

San Gabriel

San Luis Obispo

Presidio of Monterey

San Francisco Bay

Tubac

Culiacán

Guadalajara

Mexico City

Gulf
of
Mexico

12

they left. I can still hear Mama telling the story about the baby and scolding the poor soul who had brought his wife in that condition. But for everyone else, it was a safe journey. For my grandparents, there was no doubt it was Captain Anza and God who had kept them safe.

Six long months after they left, they arrived at the Monterey Presidio, the closest settlement to their new home. Back in Culiacán, it was sunny and hot every day, but Monterey was so much farther north and so close to the ocean that it was almost always foggy and cold. It rained almost every day, and if it wasn't raining, it was cloudy and gray. The settlers hated Monterey. The flour for the tortillas molded, and many people caught chest colds and coughed for weeks. Grandmama used up much of her precious herb collection helping people get rid of those sick chests.

Worse yet, they had to stay in Monterey for almost three months waiting to go the last 100 miles of their journey.

The quarters they had to stay in didn't help their mood. The buildings inside the presidio were hardly buildings at all. They were huts made of pine poles and mud with sod roofs. Water dripped through that sod night and day, just like water out of a soaked sponge. Sometimes they slept inside one of these houses. Other times they slept on the ground in a tent or a kind of lean-to with a thatched roof. Everything was wet even if it wasn't raining. Sometimes the firewood was so damp they could not light a fire to cook or to warm themselves.

The only bright spot for Mama was the mission at Carmel. Often she and Grandmama rode there to attend **mass** or to help Father Serra. Even as a young girl, Mama sensed there was something special about the little man

They had to stay in Monterey for almost three months.

14

who started all the missions. Grandmama told her that they were honored and blessed to help him.

Grandmama Tapia taught the Indian women her way of sewing and cooking, and she learned from them about the herbs that grew in California. Mama played with the **neophyte** children. Neophytes were Christianized Indians who lived at the missions.

Time passed and the settlers began to wonder if they would ever get to their new home. They began worrying that their supplies would not last. And they worried that the seeds and small trees they brought from Culiacán would not live in this foggy, wet place.

While my grandparents waited and worried at the Monterey Presidio, they became friends with a young soldier named Marcos Briones who was stationed there. Marcos, of course, would become my papa many years later! However, at that time in Monterey, he was an optimistic and adventurous young man, who usually helped lift everyone's spirits with his booming voice and happy ways. But as the days wore on, even his smile had disappeared.

You see, Papa had come to Monterey several years earlier to help protect California for the king. But in his heart of hearts, what he really hoped for was to be paid for his services in land. You see, he had a dream, too. It was to own his own land! Of course he and Mama were not married yet, but when he did marry, he wanted a good life with a home and land to give to his children. In New Spain only rich people owned land, and Papa was poor. But he dreamed that California would change that for him. He planned to go to San Francisco Bay with Anza's settlers and get his own land. Now he too worried there would be no supplies left to support the new settlement.

Just when things were at their worst, a great miracle happened. Papa and the Tapias were walking along the ocean one day, talking about all the bad things they were afraid of. Suddenly, as if God heard their fears, small fish began to throw themselves on the beach. They watched in amazement and began to count until they could not count fast enough. Great piles of fish lay all about them. They couldn't walk without stepping on them. They were small fish, yes, but so many!

For the next 23 days the grunion, as they were called, landed on the beach. All the Spanish women joined the Indian women gathering the fish and drying them. Drying fish was not an easy task in that soggy climate, but Grandmama watched the Indian women and learned how to do it. For a while, at least, her worries about starving were over.

The miracle of the fish put a smile back on Papa's face. That first night during prayers, all the soldiers and settlers gave thanks for those small silvery fish and for the bounty of the new land. The fish proved to them that God would not bring them this far without providing for them.

———

When Papa finished a story, sometimes he liked to tell us what we children should have learned from it. This story, he explained, taught two very important lessons. First, be willing to learn new ways from others, no matter how different they may seem from you, just like Grandmama had learned to dry fish from the Indian women. And second, always express thanks to God for all gifts, small or large, expected or not. Papa taught us to live by these lessons, and because of them, our family never lacked food or honor. ❧

A New Home at Last

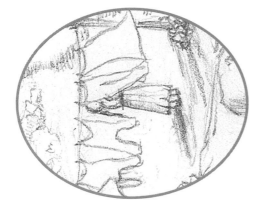

The day finally came when they were allowed to move on to their new home. Everyone cheered! Grandpapa Tapia even fired his gun into the air. But the bitter came with the sweet. The group of settlers was being split up. Half were going to San Francisco, but the other half would go to Santa Clara to build a new mission there. How bad they felt to lose these friends with whom they had been through so much! Everyone promised that they would visit when they could, and off they went.

Now I would like to tell you that Papa said all was well when they reached the site of their new home, but that would not be true. Just like Monterey, the fog rolled in and out, and it was damp and cold. When they arrived, there was not even a sod roof to cover their heads or a stick wall to keep out the wind. There were some good things, and optimistic Papa, of course, looked for them.

The very good news was that there were springs everywhere so that drinking water was no problem. There was firewood for cooking, but timber for building was only available at a great distance. Grass was abundant for the horses and cattle, and best of all for Grandmama, there were herbs in great supply. She set to restocking her medicines almost the minute she arrived.

From the hill where they planned to build the presidio, they could see baby whales, dolphins, and seals playing in the bay. There was also a river they called the Arroyo de Dolores flowing nearby, and it had enough water to operate a mill, or at least they thought so at first.

Right away the settlers began building a chapel. None of the soldiers were skilled craftsmen, but they worked hard. They had only the tools they brought with them, but all the men had strong arms and backs, and they did the best job they could with what they had. Even Mama and the other children helped. After they finished the chapel, they built walls of wooden stakes and **tules** to form the presidio. The walls were supposed to protect them in case they were attacked by the Russians, the English, or unfriendly Indians. Inside the presidio walls the settlers built warehouses, a guardhouse, and barracks for the soldiers and their families. Papa's chest always puffed up with pride when he told us about his part in building all these places in the northernmost corner of New Spain. He felt honored to help.

You might wonder if the buildings Mama and her family lived in were any better than those in Monterey. Unfortunately they weren't. Lumber was too hard to get to build houses of wood. The clay in the earth was so poor that the adobe bricks they tried to make melted in the rain. Mama and the others ended up again in soggy little mud and stick huts. What else could they do? They had no way to return to Culiacán. They had to make the best of where they were.

Not long after they finished the presidio, they began building the mission. It was named Mission San Francisco de Asis, for St. Francis, but they called it simply Mission Dolores after the nearby river. Dolores means sorrows in Spanish. There were days when they thought that name a perfect one.

Nine years passed. Mama grew up and married Papa when she was 13. That was considered old enough in those days. Although my parents wished they could settle down, Papa was sent to help at many other missions, and Mama followed. Together they lived in tumble-down houses wherever Papa was stationed. The only good times Mama remembered were when they visited their old friends at Mission Santa Clara. They danced the old dances and talked of home where it was always warm and dry.

Times were hard. Papa had a small salary, but the money had to come all the way from Mexico City. Sometimes it didn't make it. My mama made a little money washing clothes and sewing or embroidering, but there was never any extra. At times they had to depend on the missions for food, or Papa had to go bear hunting to keep them from starving.

It helped a little that all the soldiers and settlers were in the same boat. Mama said she would have liked a house of adobe that didn't melt, a roof that didn't leak, and some furniture. All she and Papa had were a stool and some grass mats, no bed or chairs. But one day Mama had the honor to visit the *comandante's* wife at the San Francisco pre-

They lived in tumble-down houses wherever Papa was stationed.

sidio. When she went inside, Mama saw the *comandante's* wife sitting cross-legged on a grass mat in the middle of a dirt floor. Mama could hardly believe her eyes. She decided right then that if this elegant lady in her fine silk dress could make do with so little, Mama could too.

Mama and Papa worked hard, and Papa still dreamed of owning land. Mama told him an old Spanish saying—*"El sueña es alimento de los pobres.* Dreams are food of the poor." But he smiled and said, *"Quien con la esperanza vive, alegre muere.* He who lives with hope, dies happy." Papa still had hope, but most of the other soldiers did not.

In all those years since they had arrived in Alta California, only 20 families received land grants. They were, of course, already rich people. The missions owned the best land, but they kept it for the **indios.** There seemed to be no rewards for the soldiers and families who traveled so far. Some soldiers talked badly about the padres. Some wanted to seize land from the king for themselves. The soldiers had worked hard for Spain, and they thought they deserved their own small rancho as a reward. But the king said, "No."

So you see, Alta California did not fulfill Papa's dream. After he married Mama and we were born, he realized he would never be a landowner. But Papa was not one to stay disappointed for long. He simply changed his dream. "You children are the real treasures of my life," he said. "Someday you will own part of California." When I first heard him say that, I made a very unusual vow for a girl. I swore that one day I would own my own land. I would! I would make Papa's dream come true. ❧

21

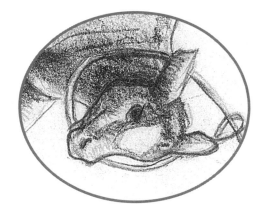

Villa de Branciforte

Before I tell you about my life, I will tell you about Papa's last hope for land. In 1797, five years before I was born, the king of Spain was concerned again that a foreign country might invade Alta California. This time he feared England. He wanted more Spanish settlers to come here, just as my grandparents had come with Captain Anza. This time the king planned to build a grand pueblo, or town, north of Monterey to attract new settlers. He agreed to spend ten times as much money as he had on the Anza expedition. This new pueblo was called Villa de Branciforte, and it was supposed to be a model for future pueblos.

When Papa saw the plans for Branciforte, his spirits soared. It was a wonderful design! Not like the poor presidios at all. It would be a real town with nice adobes built around a central plaza. At last the Briones family would live in a fine adobe house with a good roof, and they would have land and cattle of their own. Papa was retired from the army by then, and he was free to move where he wanted. His old dream might come true after all! He volunteered immediately.

Eagerly Mama and Papa moved to Branciforte and waited for the town to develop. But before long, they noticed something was wrong. The fine neighbors they expected—skilled carpenters, masons, tailors, and other artisans—never arrived. No one of quality wanted to come to Branciforte. Perhaps they heard how bad the weather was or that the government was not living up to its promises to build fine houses. Only the very poor wanted to come, and not even many of them. The government was so desperate that they ended up sending criminals from Guadalajara!

Mama could not believe her bad fortune. Branciforte filled with gamblers, drinkers, and thieves. Soon it was known all over Alta California as a place to avoid. The governor of California complained to the **viceroy** in Mexico City that the residents of Branciforte were a scandal. The padres complained bitterly that the pueblo set a bad example for the neophytes. Sometimes we even had trouble visiting my parents' old friends in San Jose because the mayor didn't want anyone from Branciforte in his town.

How do you think Mama and Papa felt? They knew they were not people of means, but they were people of good reputation. Mama wanted to leave, but Papa was appointed ***comisionado*** of Branciforte. Papa hoped he could improve the town, and he gave it all he had. He tried to make the residents follow the laws, but they were poor and desperate and bitter. The government had promised them a better life too, and the promises were not kept.

Let me give you an example of how the people of Branciforte misbehaved. One day when I was about 15, Father Olbez at Mission Santa Cruz, Branciforte's nearest mission, looked out his window and saw the pirate ship of Henri Bouchard anchored in the bay. Bouchard had already attacked Monterey, and the padre had been warned he was coming toward Santa Cruz and Branciforte. The padre alerted the residents of Branciforte, and then rode to Santa Clara to be safe.

Just as he was leaving, he packed up the valuables of the mission—the candlesticks, the statues, and his vestments—all those sacred things. He asked some people from Branciforte to carry them to Santa Clara for him. That was a mistake, of course. What did we see when we were heading to Santa Clara ourselves but those men riding toward San Francisco with the church's property. We heard they sold all those precious objects to sailors from the foreign ships!

Mama was never happy at Branciforte. She took the only course of action she knew. She took us to Santa Clara to visit friends as often as she could, and every Sunday we spent the day at Mission Santa Cruz to get away from what she called "that terrible place." ❧

My Childhood

For Mama and Papa, Branciforte was awful, but for us children it wasn't so bad. I was born there in 1802. We children never noticed people gambling or drinking. We were too busy working hard all day, every-day. We had no school nearby and no idea we were miss-ing anything. No one we knew could read or write except for the padres.

But we did learn. Mama made sure that all of us knew how to do everything that was needed to keep a house and family going. I knew how to cut and sew a soldier's leather jacket and to embroider a pretty dress. I made soap good enough to sell, and our candles were often used at the mission. I could rope a cow and tan a hide, just as my brothers could sew shoes and cook if they had to. We were prepared to take care of ourselves. In spite of Mama's fears, we grew up to be responsible citizens. Mama and Papa were proud of us and told us often that we were the gold California brought them.

Papa built a nice herd of cattle. He borrowed cows from the mission. Then, when they had calves, he returned the borrowed ones and kept the babies. As the herd grew, it became our best source of trade goods. We even had two or three cows close to the house so we could milk them and trade the fresh milk for goods we couldn't make.

In those days we had no fences. Our cattle ran together on open range with everyone else's. Every spring we branded the hide of each new calf or placed a marker on its ear so we could tell who owned which cattle. When Papa gave me my first horse, Platita, a beautiful golden horse with a silvery white mane and tail, I was about as happy as a **Californio** could be. At seven or eight, I could ride all day herding cattle with my older brothers, Gregorio and Felipe.

My favorite place in those days was Santa Clara because of Father Catala who was the priest there. We children loved him. He was a very devout priest, but he was also mischievous in some ways. At that time it was not thought proper for a priest to ride a horse, but Father Catala loved horses. The other padres scolded him and said he should sit with dignity in a wagon. He just told them, "I am but a poor Franciscan who was brought up in the saddle. I must ride." I loved riding with Father Catala, as far and as fast as we could go!

After a while, I learned to rope. At first I could only throw the lasso around the calf's neck, but by the time I was ten or eleven, I threw the calf to the ground just about as well as my brothers. I never did learn to bulldog, like Gregorio and Papa. That was flipping a calf by yanking hard on its tail. But my brothers liked to stand back and applaud their little sister Juanita when I roped!

My brothers liked to applaud their little sister Juanita when I roped!

When they were first married, Mama and Papa smuggled any extra goods they had to foreign ships. The king told them not to trade with anyone except Spaniards, but Mama and Papa didn't listen. If they had, they might have starved, and where would we be now?

In Branciforte, we slipped goods to the ships that came to the ports. Whichever one of us sneaked to the ships to sell our extra hides and milk had to be careful. I have to admit that when it was my turn, if there was a spare penny left, I'd buy something dear. The ships were full of small treasures, like candy and ribbons and beautiful shoes. I might buy a ribbon, and Papa never complained.

The best break from our regular work was the rodeo. The word comes from the Spanish *rodear* which means roundup. How we loved them! They happened twice a year, and we children waited for them the same way we waited for candy. Mostly it was a time for work, branding in spring and butchering in the fall, but we also had great **fiestas** after the hard work was done. The rodeos gave young men a chance to show young women their fancy roping and bronco riding skills. Their ability to attract a wife depended a lot on these skills, and many a wedding match was made at a rodeo.

Sometimes after the contests, the men played games. One of the favorite games was having a **vaquero** gallop as fast as he could and pull a chicken out of the ground after someone buried it up to its neck in dirt. Papa and Gregorio often tried their hand at it, but they never had the heart to pull the poor thing out of the hole and risk yanking its head off. They just tapped the chicken on the beak and rode on by, leaning down so far that their hats touched the ground. We Brioneses laughed and waved and applauded their daring! It was such fun.

The fall roundup was the dirtiest. That's when we had the *matanza* or slaughtering. No one liked this work, but it had to be done. Sticky blood splattered all over us and collected clouds of flies, and the poor cattle bawled so pitifully. But slaughtering was part of rancho life. Much of what we traded or used for ourselves came from the cattle. We wasted nothing from their meat to their fat and hides. We even used their horns on top of walls and fences to make them taller.

After the cattle were killed, the *peladores*, or skinners, came in first to take off the hides. Next came the *tasajeros* who cut up the meat so it could be dried. Then the women gathered the fat in leather hampers and took it to be melted in large iron or copper kettles. What a hot, messy, smelly job it was! It took us days. We sold most of the tallow we made to the **Yankee** traders and made soap and candles from the rest. Our willingness to work like this could mean the difference between eating and not eating the following winter.

Sometimes *matanzas* were made even more difficult by the grizzly bears that lived in Alta California in the old days. There were so many around Branciforte that Mama wouldn't leave the house without a large knife in her hand. You know a bear has a nose that can smell across many miles, and the smell of blood drew them like flies. When a bear became too bold and got too close to the meat, some of the *vaqueros* would jump on their horses and run them off.

One time Papa and two of his friends wanted to get rid of three bears that had become particularly troublesome. They tracked them for a while and were about to dig a deep pit to trap them in, when they suddenly came upon the bears eating berries on a hillside. The bears smelled them and turned to attack. My papa and his friends grabbed their *reatas* and each roped a bear. Sometimes *vaqueros* roped bears and brought them back to the ranchos alive, just for fun, but not this time. Their horses—so well trained from working with cattle—were nervous, but they held steady against the pull of the bears. Each man slit the throat of his bear in one quick strike.

How our eyes widened when Papa told this story! We imagined him face to face with a bear twice his size, and we shivered. I'm guessing he exaggerated just a bit. A bear story had a way of getting bigger and scarier every time someone told it. But we never complained! ❧

Our Wedding

As we children grew up, Mama and Papa expected my brothers to join the army and my sisters and me to marry. By the time my brother Gregorio was 19, he was a soldier stationed at the Presidio of San Francisco. My sister Guadalupe married a soldier and lived at Polin Springs near the San Francisco Presidio.

Guadalupe had many babies very quickly, and I often stayed with her to help with the children. During one of my visits, I met my future husband, Apolinario Miranda, who was a soldier with Gregorio. He caught my eye right away because he was so handsome. I was not much different then from any other young girl who puts great value on a fine appearance.

In those days, when a young man liked a young woman, he came to her home, stood outside the front door, and sang sweet songs to her. It was called serenading. I was happy when Apolinario came to serenade me one mild winter evening. I thought he had a beautiful voice.

Guadalupe's husband, Mr. Miramontes, stood there watching him closely, for, of course, I could never be left unchaperoned with Apolinario.

When he was in the middle of his second song, all of a sudden Guadalupe's husband shouted, "Bear!" We turned around to see a grizzly sauntering toward us, as if he wanted to hear the song too. Apolinario stopped singing, jumped on his horse, and chased after the bear. I never saw anyone ride like that before! When he returned, he finished the song he had been singing, and then he sang another one, just as if nothing had happened!

Until that serenade, I hadn't given marriage much thought. Mama feared I was already past marrying age. I was nearly 18, and remember she was only 13 when she married Papa. I liked my life as it was—helping my sister and riding Platita when I could. And there was still my vow to own my own land. But this young soldier caught my attention.

When Apolinario came one day to speak to Papa, I knew immediately that he had come to ask for my hand in marriage. I wasn't sure I was ready, but when Papa gave Apolinario his permission to marry me, I did not think I could refuse. We set our wedding day for May 14, 1820, at Mission Dolores. Apolinario had hardly finished his proposal before I began sewing to prepare the goods I would need to start a new household.

In those days, if a bride was especially honored, her husband-to-be made her wedding shoes. Because we didn't have many **cobblers** in Alta California, most men could sew a leather shoe if they had to, but to make satin slippers with delicate stitches demanded a finer touch. Did Apolinario have this touch? Did he love me enough to fuss with these little shoes? I waited and waited for him to ask for a pattern of my feet. I had given up hope when about two weeks before the wedding, he sent a friend to trace their outlines. Even then I wasn't sure he would have time to finish the shoes. His army duties took him away from the presidio for days on end.

For the wedding, my entire family stayed with my sister Guadalupe near Mission Dolores. I awoke on my wedding day to find the soggy fog and clouds had split apart to let the sun stream through! This was a lucky day for us!

I dressed carefully. I was about to put on the best pair of shoes I owned when Guadalupe shouted, "Surprise!" and handed me a beautiful pair of satin shoes. Apolinario had made them after all! They fit perfectly. The rest of the day I let them peek out from under my long dress as often as I could to show my new husband how proud I was of his work.

The wedding procession started at Guadalupe's house. All the soldiers from the presidio were in dress uniforms, and their prancing horses were decorated with colorful sashes, silver buckles, and silk ribbons. The men sang as we made our way to the mission. Papa and I rode behind the soldiers on Platita. As was the custom, Papa sat behind the saddle on a bear skin rug used only for wedding processions. I rode in the saddle in front of him with my satin shoes in special stirrups made of golden braid.

Bells were ringing as we arrived at the mission. We had decorated it inside with wild flowers and brightly colored pieces of cloth. When Apolinario and I knelt at the altar to receive the final blessing, the padre wound a gold sash with silk tassels around our necks. This told people that Apolinario and I were bound together as man and wife.

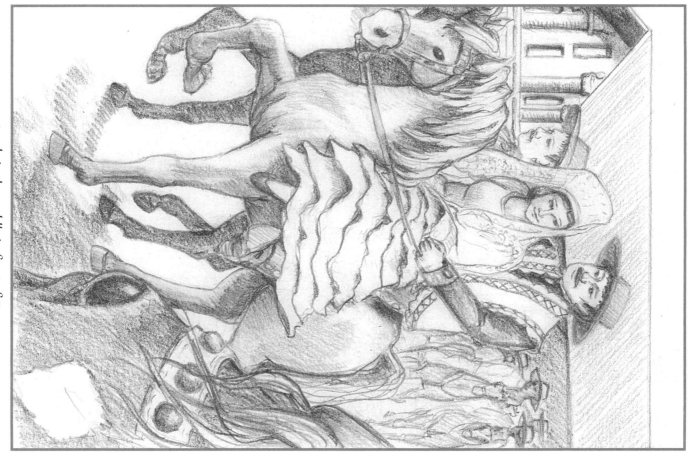

I rode in the saddle in front of Papa.

Our wedding party lasted for days. People came from all over, Carmel, Santa Clara, and Santa Cruz, Monterey, and San Jose. They stayed with friends or pitched tents in the fields near the presidio. It doesn't seem possible that we could sing and dance for three whole days without sleeping, but we certainly tried. We Californios love fiestas, and a wedding is a perfect excuse for one. We spread food out on the tables, and the dance floor filled with twirling dancers. Apolinario showed off his light, twirling steps and elegant stomps while the rest of us clapped. Then Papa placed a cup of water on his head and performed *la bamba* without spilling a drop. As the fiesta went on, some people slept while others danced. Then those who had been eating and dancing changed places with those who had been sleeping.

Finally, when our feet were so sore we could hardly walk, someone said, "It is time for the Mirandas to begin their new life." We kissed each guest on both cheeks and walked the short distance to our small quarters in the presidio.

I was a married woman. ❧

Life at the San Francisco Presidio

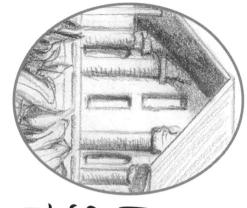

had heard Mama and Papa tell how hard life had been for them in the early days at the presidios, but I was used to the relatively good life at Branciforte. At least we had our own cattle and enough to eat. At the presidio, Apolinario and I started with nothing, and things turned out to be worse for us than they had been for Mama and Papa.

From 1810 to 1820, the ten years before we were married, Spain did not send any money or supplies to the soldiers in Alta California. New Spain was trying to win its independence from the Spanish king, and the king was too busy fighting wars to think of us in Alta California. Apolinario had not received any salary, and the presidio buildings themselves were falling down. No one had made any repairs for years. The cannons were so rusty they would not fire, and there was no powder to fire them anyway. In truth, we were just about forgotten.

At first, we built our own little hut near Guadalupe at Polin Springs. We thought of that spring as Briones territory. Our house was a crumbly little place. We made the walls of sticks and filled the holes with mud to keep the wind out. I wove branches together to make a roof. Like my grandparents, I tried to make tiles for the roof, but they disintegrated. In the winter I cooked inside. During the summer I cooked under a *ramada* I built. We slept on mats I wove from tule reeds. I made our clothes, Apolinario's uniforms, candles, soap—the things Mama had taught me to do. We were luckier than many of our friends who did not know how to do for themselves. For most things, they had to rely on the padres at the mission and all the neophyte Indians who worked in the fields and workshops for the padres.

Our children began arriving, and we needed more room. We would have eight altogether, three boys and five girls. We built a better house at Ojo de Agua Figueroa, another spring near the presidio. There were so few people and so much land that we could pick just about any place we wanted to build a house. We didn't have any legal rights to the house or the land, but at first, that didn't matter. Later, it would matter a great deal.

We had two rooms downstairs and a loft upstairs where we stored food. We made the walls of adobe and the roof of tile. How proud I was when I finally found good clay! Just like Papa we started our own herd from the mission stock. We built a corral for the few cows we tamed to milk, and the rest grazed on open land near the presidio. We also fenced off an area to keep the cattle and horses out of our vegetable garden, and we planted a small orchard of trees that grew in that climate. I was young, and I knew how to work. I didn't mind because I was making a better life for our family. Even without Apolinario's salary, we managed.

In 1821, New Spain won its independence from the King of Spain and became Mexico. Suddenly we were Mexican citizens instead of Spaniards. It didn't make any difference, though. Mexico was poor and couldn't help us either. But, at least as Mexicans we could legally trade with the many Yankee ships that anchored in San Francisco Bay. We didn't have to sneak to them the way we did in Branciforte. Trading became our way of life. We had things like fresh fruit, vegetables, and milk that the Yankees wanted. They had needles and sugar and other things that we could not make or raise for ourselves. And they had such fine dresses and shoes! How I loved to look at those silk dresses and imagine what it might be like to wear such a fancy dress!

Because of the trading, our family's life improved steadily, but life for the soldiers got worse. When Mariano Guadalupe Vallejo became *comandante* of the presidio in 1830, ten years after we were married, the soldiers hoped that he would get their back pay and some new equipment for the presidio. He was well respected and a good and fair man. He requested money and supplies from the Mexican government, but he heard nothing. Comandante Vallejo asked again and again for help, but sadly the new government of Mexico did not respond.

Finally, he asked if he could sell the few remaining buildings of the presidio to get some money for Apolinario and the other men. Still he heard nothing. When the rains took all except two or three buildings, the *comandante* made his own decision. He decided to move the soldiers and cattle north to Sonoma where the weather was better and more crops would grow. Apolinario didn't know what to do.

Before the *comandante* left, I got Apolinario to ask him for a land grant to Ojo de Agua Figueroa. I knew that we might lose everything we were so proud of—the house, the orchard, and the corral—if we did not have a title. The best we could hope for was a provisional grant, and the *comandante* gave us one. It was in Apolinario's name, of course. Still I felt some part of this small rancho was mine and that I was closer to fulfilling Papa's dream.

Only two or three soldiers and their families stayed behind when Vallejo moved the men to Sonoma. Apolinario was one of them, and this was the beginning of his ruin. He was near retirement and did not want to move. He had been promoted to corporal, but without pay, the promotion meant nothing. After a while, he lost all hope of ever getting what was due him, and he began drinking. He was not a bad man, but his worst days and mine were beginning and our happy ones ending.

I could have forgiven him his taste for **aguardiente,** but he kept poor company and failed to provide for the family. This was an insult to all of us. We worked. Apolinario drank with his rough friends, and I could not bear it. I kept hearing Mama reciting one of her **dichos,** *"Dieme con quien andas y te diere quien eres.* Tell me who you run around with, and I'll tell you who you are." I did not like to think that Apolinario was becoming like the men he ran around with, but he was. He set such a bad example for the children that I didn't want to be around him. I did not want my sons or daughters to see the man their father had become.

The Alta California of Juana Briones

Pacific Ocean

Monterey Bay

San Francisco Bay

San Francisco Presidio

Mission San Francisco

Yerba Buena

Rancho La Purisima Concepción

Mission Santa Clara

Branciforte

Mission Santa Cruz

Mission San Jose

Monterey Presidio

Mission Carmel

Slowly I began to move to Yerba Buena Cove on San Francisco Bay. There were two houses there already, and that's where the Yankee ships that I traded with anchored. Every day I traveled there with my cart filled with goods to sell. It made sense for my children and me to build a small home there. The presidio was no longer the center of our lives, and we could get away from Apolinario and his friends.

I never imagined that house would become part of a new pueblo called Yerba Buena. And then, when the Yankees took over, Yerba Buena turned into the wild city of San Francisco. I certainly did not know I was starting anything like that!

Our move to Yerba Buena marked the beginning of our new life and our independence. It was an exciting time for everyone! ❧

A New World

It was also a frightening time. First the new Mexican government ignored us. Then they turned our world upside down. They passed what they called **secularization** laws to force the padres to give up the land they held for the neophyte Indians. The government said they wanted to make a better life for the Indians and to open up land for more settlers. But that's not the way it turned out. Governor Figueroa did break up the mission lands, and they did initially go to some of the neophytes and some Mexican citizens. But eventually, a few rich families ended up with the largest amounts of land. Life was better for only a very few.

The mission padres like Father Catala were left with only their church and a small home. Without the neophytes, they had no one left to repair the mission buildings or to garden and make the goods that helped care for the settlers and the Indians. Many of our friends relied on the missions for food and other supplies. For them, secularization was a disaster.

But secularization was hardest on the Indians. They received small grants of mission lands, but they were often tricked out of them or gambled them away. Those Indians born at the missions no longer knew how to hunt and gather like their ancestors had, so they couldn't live in the old way. To survive after they lost their land, they had to work as *vaqueros* for the very Californios who had taken their land from them. The Indians were fine *vaqueros*, the very best! Their treatment seemed so unfair!

I cannot tell you how terribly these things upset me. There was little I could do to right the wrongs, but I did adopt our dear Cecilia, an Indian girl from Mission Santa Clara. I had doctored her parents when they were dying in a measles epidemic. I would have taken in more children, but I had so many of my own to care for and no help from my husband.

As I worked in Yerba Buena—thankful that I didn't have to rely on the mission—I often heard Papa whispering in my ear, "Be willing to learn new ways from others." With this advice, I learned how to be a good businesswoman. I learned who to trust and not to trust. I watched the Yankee traders just as my grandmother had watched the Indian women so many years earlier. I learned what the Yankees wanted most for trade and how to strike a good bargain with them. We had the freshest food in Yerba Buena, and I expected to be paid adequately for it. I treated my customers fairly and offered them hospitality. I did my business with kindness and good will as Papa had taught me.

One of my best Yankee teachers was Mr. Richardson, the harbormaster of Yerba Buena. He was a fine businessman and good friend. He had the first house near the ships' landing in the cove. It was a meager house made of redwood posts and old canvas from the sail of one of his ships.

How we laughed when we went inside and felt the wind lift the sides of that funny house! We thought we were at sea!

Mr. Richardson helped us build our first house, partly wood and partly canvas. I started a second garden, and we brought the dairy cows down from Ojo de Agua so that the milk would be even fresher when I sold it. We worked from first light to after dark. There were cows to milk, herbs to gather, weeds to pull, vegetables to plant and pick, tea to brew, guests to be cared for, and babies to be tended.

Everyone had a job. The first thing my little ones learned when they could walk was how to pull weeds and load the wagon. The girls and I did the sailors' laundry, and we mended their clothes. We did so much laundry that Mr. Richardson called the area where we laundered, Washerwoman's Lagoon! My daughters Presentación and Manuela were fine seamstresses, and they did some of the sewing. Jesus went to the boats to see what the men needed, and he delivered goods and messages for me.

By 1841, we had replaced that funny little canvas house with a brand new adobe. It was large enough for me to rent rooms. After a while we added outbuildings and fenced corrals, and even made an adobe wall around the whole area.

I asked the *alcalde* for more land near our new house to make a bigger garden, but he refused to give it to me without my husband's approval. Apolinario spent very little time with us by then. He was still drinking and had become abusive. I almost considered myself an unmarried woman, but in the eyes of the law I was still married. Even though I wanted nothing to do with my husband, I had to go to him and ask for his help. Apolinario agreed to ask for the extra land, and the *alcalde* granted it to him immediately.

We worked from first light until after dark.

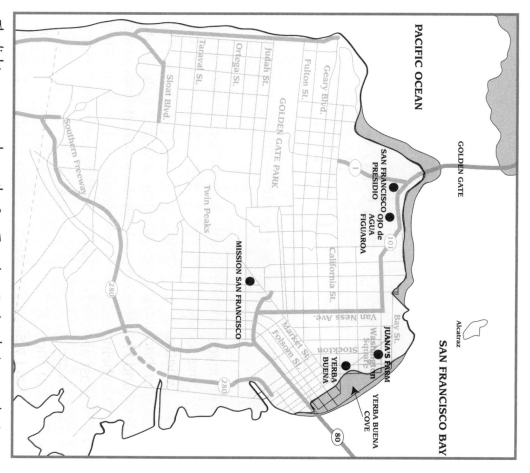

The light gray area shows the San Francisco Peninsula in Juana's time. The dark gray at the peninsula's upper edge shows where land was added to make modern San Francisco.

As soon as I heard the land was ours, the children and I began building a new, larger garden. We brought down more cows and had a regular little dairy in Yerba Buena. We were truly independent at last! ❧

Aid and Comfort

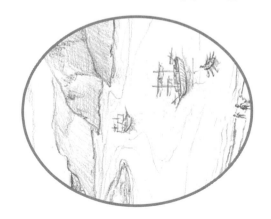

Whoever answered the door of our home at the cove could tell by the look on the visitor's face whether to set out tea or to gather my medicines. My mother had taught me all she knew about herbs and healing, and I had become known as a **curandera.** I came as close to being a doctor as anyone in Yerba Buena. There were almost always sick people staying at our little house, and they were welcome to stay until they were well. I also traveled to the homes of those too sick to come to me. Sometimes I visited the Indian villages to help old friends. Papa and Mama had taught me to help those in need, and I used my medicines willingly without pay. How proud I am that my brother Gregorio's son Pablo continued the family tradition by becoming a doctor.

My favorite part of doctoring was being a midwife. I loved to watch the arrival of a new being, and I always went gladly when someone came in the small hours of the night to call me to a birthing.

But it wasn't only the sick that needed help. One day when we were still at Ojo de Agua, I went down to a ship to sell milk to the captain. As I left, a young sailor named Mr. Brown motioned me to follow him behind a pile of cattle hides where no one could see us. In a whisper, he asked if I would be willing to help him and three other men. With nothing more than a nod of my head, I said yes. I knew what he wanted. He wanted to **jump ship.**

The lives of the sailors were awful. Many had been taken from their homes on the East Coast of America when they were boys and forced to work for little food and little pay on the dirty, dangerous ships. These men had dreams, too, like my parents and grandparents. They wanted to stay in California, but their captains controlled them with iron fists. If they were caught jumping ship, they were severely punished.

That night I had just blown out the lantern when I heard noises outside the house. The children were sound asleep. I stepped outside to find Mr. Brown and three other men. I hid them in the loft for a few days until I could arrange their escape.

I had to be careful and not let anyone outside the family know we were helping the sailors. The captain of the ship was offering a reward for them, and the families near the presidio were so poor, I was afraid they'd turn in the sailors for the reward.

I developed a plan. One dark night, I hid the men in a cart, and my daughter Presentación and I hauled them to my brother Felipe's small fishing boat. Once along the way, a guard stopped us. We told him we were going night fishing. The guard looked at our cart and saw fishing poles sticking out from under a canvas. He let us go. Little did he know there were four men crouching under that canvas. When we reached the boat, my brother took the men to his rancho across the bay. They stayed there until after their ship had sailed.

That was not the last we saw of them. One of the men returned to us several times in later years when he was injured or sick so I could doctor him. Mr. Brown lived with us a few years later and became an important ally when we needed him. He testified in our behalf with the Americans when we had to prove ownership of our land at the presidio.

These were not the last men we helped. Many fine people who became important in developing San Francisco were deserters from those Yankee ships. They saw the promise California offered, and they left their old lives to seize it.

Not everything we did was dangerous or serious. We liked a practical joke now and then too. We played a good one on two young cabin boys, a Mr. Thomes and a Mr. Lewey, who visited the bay in 1843 aboard one of the Yankee ships. They came to the house one day asking for milk for their captain. They were mischievous-looking boys, so I decided to have some fun with them.

I told Pedro, my ranch hand, to bring over one of the milking cows. He dragged her out of the pen away from her calf and tied her to a stump with her hind legs and tail strapped together. Our cattle were nearly wild, and we had to restrain them like that to keep from being kicked into the bay!

I winked at Pedro and he brought out a chamber pot from the house. You know *chamber pot* is the word the Yankees give to the pot you use in the middle of the night when it is too cold and too far to walk to the outhouse. We decided to let those boys think we were putting fresh milk into a used chamber pot. We had just bought a new one, but they didn't know that. We wanted to see what they would do.

Well, those boys nearly died of laughter. The short one saw the pot first, and he held up his hand as if to stop me. But then he whispered to his mate, who started to laugh. While I milked, they laughed so hard one finally fell off the fence.

When the "pail" was full, the one who fell off the fence went into the house with Cecilia. He came back with a tin pan from the kitchen and asked if I would fill it. I asked what was wrong with the pail I was using, but he said nothing. He just begged me to fill that tin with milk for him and his friend to drink. I asked him again what was wrong with the pot, but still he said nothing. The two of them went off carrying the full chamber pot and the small tin they were drinking from.

As it turned out, years later one of them wrote a book about his travels, and he mentioned this experience. Presentación read me the book, so I finally understood why those boys didn't stop me. The truth is they were playing a joke too.

They didn't like their captain, and they thought he deserved milk from a dirty chamber pot! I thought that was pretty funny until Presentación read that the boys thought Californios were so simple-minded that we didn't know any better than to use an old chamber pot for milk! Imagine! If I had known what they were thinking, I would have given them an earful! ❧

A Rancho At Last!

The last of my stories takes place in 1844. That year I took the saddest step of my life. I asked the **bishop** in Santa Barbara to grant me a legal separation from Apolinario. This decision was against everything I knew about the holy sacrament of marriage. But my husband's behavior became so cruel that I could no longer allow him near us. His bad reputation was well known, and the bishop never doubted the truth of my complaints. He took no time at all in granting me the separation. After that, people called me the Widow Briones, and I did not stop them. In my mind, I had become a widow long before Apolinario died in 1847.

But sadness can be accompanied by great blessings if one is fortunate, and I was very fortunate. By 1844, I had saved enough money from my trading to buy a rancho. I was no longer considered a married woman, and I could finally own land myself! I could fulfill my vow and Papa's dream! For $300, I bought Rancho La Purisima

Concepción, this 4,000 acres of beautiful rolling land with rivers and springs where we gather today. As a child, I had ridden over this glorious place with my brothers, and I knew it the way I know my own children. I purchased it from my old friends Jose Gorgonio and his son Jose Ramon, two Santa Clara Mission Indians. They were two of the lucky ones who had been able to keep their land and then sell it for a good price. I was even luckier to be able to buy it from them.

To do it just right, I planned carefully. Since the mission lands had been divided, people squabbled constantly over who owned what. Often they went to court to try to steal land, or they just squatted on someone else's property until they got chased off. I was worried because, since I could not read or write, I had to trust other people to make sure the papers were correct. Fortunately, Papa had taught me to size people up, and I was good at deciding who was trustworthy and who wasn't. When all my papers were in order, I went to the most powerful men in California.

First, I requested permission from the governor to make the purchase. Then, I received authorization from the secretary of state to appear before the mayor in San Jose, which was the nearest town to the new rancho. The mayor authorized the sale, and at last I had the land Papa wanted for us when he came to California almost eighty years before! I had made his dream come true. I cannot tell you how happy that made me!

For a while, we lived between two homes again, traveling between Yerba Buena and Rancho La Purisima. But by 1849, when all that foolishness of the Gold Rush took over life in Yerba Buena, I had moved permanently to the rancho. Thousands of people from all over the world had

I had made Papa's dream come true. How happy that made me!

rushed into Yerba Buena at that time, and I was too old to want to take part in that craziness, getting rich one day and losing everything the next.

A friend of Papa's told his son, "God has given this gold to the Americans. Had he desired us Californios to have it, he would have given it to us before now." Our gold came from what we could grow on the rich California soil. At the rancho we plant our fields and tend our livestock. We work hard everyday because that is the Briones way. I still care for the sick and welcome visitors with a cup of tea. You children have grown up, married, and had your own children. I have no doubt that I have reaped my California gold.

I wish for no more for myself except, perhaps, that Mama and Papa had lived to see this fine rancho. It would have lived up to all their dreams.

My wish for you is that you will remember these stories from my Mama and Papa and from me, as I have told them to you today. Remember them, *mis hijos*; these stories are your stories—the history of the Briones family and the history of Alta California. ❧

Afterword

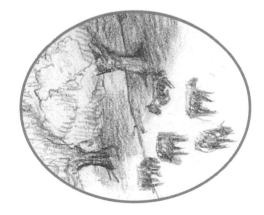

At Rancho Purisima Concepción Juana Briones surrounded herself with all she loved—her family and friends and the ranching life she dreamed of when she was a little girl in Branciforte. Gaiety and hospitality marked her home. Twice a year she held a rodeo and welcomed everyone—family, friends, and strangers. She was never happier than when her family came to visit. It was then that she told her stories.

Occasionally, she left the rancho to visit family or to help those in need. Even when she was 70 and 80 years old, she served as nurse and doctor throughout the area. Often neighbors came for her to cure those beyond curing. And no matter how late at night, she mounted her horse and rode to help.

From the rancho, she faced one major challenge. When California became part of the United States, the Californios had to prove to the American government that they had legal title to their land. Many Californios were fooled by the

new American laws and lost their property, but not Juana. In 1852, she presented her papers to the American Land Commission. The title to Ojo de Agua Figueroa, the land near the San Francisco Presidio that Comandante Vallejo had granted her husband, was challenged.

If the commission thought Juana would give up easily on a fight for land, they were wrong. With the help of American friends, she started a ten-year struggle to maintain possession of Ojo de Agua Figueroa for her children. Mr. Brown, one of the sailors she helped jump ship, testified in her behalf, as did many of the people she had been kind to in her Yerba Buena days. The battle went all the way to the United States Supreme Court, but in 1862, the court found in Juana's favor. Today, this land is near the corner of Lyon and Green Streets just outside the Presidio of San Francisco.

Juana never wanted to leave Rancho Purisima Concepción, where she spent the best years of her life. But when her health failed in the middle 1880s, her daughters persuaded her to move to nearby Mayfield to be with them. She died peacefully on December 3, 1889, at the age of 87!

She was buried the next day in the cemetery of the Church of the Nativity. No stone marks her grave. It is as she wanted it. She said that a person's life lived well should be marker enough.

Juana's Yerba Buena property, where she was the third resident of what would become San Francisco, was located where Washington Square is now in the North Beach section of San Francisco. Rancho Purisima Concepción was located in what is now Palo Alto and Los Altos Hills. Most of the land has been sold off and is now covered with modern homes and streets. Her house still stands, although it has been added to and changed by later residents. At this writing in 2001, its current owners want to tear it down or move it. They are in a battle with the government of the City of Palo Alto and other people who want to save Juana's home. To those who would save the house, it is one of the few treasures that remains to remind us of Juana Briones and all the other early California pioneers who ventured into the unknown and worked hard to fulfill their dreams. ❧

Time Line

*Not all the important dates in
Juana Briones' life are known.*

1542   Juan Rodriguez Cabrillo explores
       California coast for Spain.

1769   First mission in California established in
       San Diego.

1770   Second California mission established in
       Carmel.

1775   Juana's mother and grandparents start for
       California with Captain Anza.

1776   They arrive in California and help build
       the San Francisco Presidio.

1797   Villa de Branciforte begun.

1799   Juana's parents live in Branciforte.

1802   Juana Briones is born.

1810   New Spain goes to war with Spain to win
       its independence.

1812   Marcos Briones is *comisionado* of
       Branciforte.

1818   Pirate Henri Bouchard attacks Santa Cruz.

1820   Juana marries Apolinario Miranda.

1821   Mexico wins its independence from Spain.
       Juana and Apolinario's first child is born.

1833	Vallejo issues Apolinario a provisional grant for Ojo de Agua Figueroa.
1834	Secularization of missions begins.
1835	Juana moves to Yerba Buena.
1844	Juana legally separates from Apolinario.
	Juana receives legal title to her Yerba Buena property.
	She purchases Rancho Purisima Concepción.
1845	Juana builds a house at the new rancho.
	Mexican-American War begins.
1848	Mexico loses war. California becomes part of the United States.
1849	The Gold Rush begins.
1850	California becomes a state.
1852	Juana begins legal battle with U.S. Land Commision for Ojo de Agua Figueroa.
1862	She wins title to Ojo de Agua Figueroa for her children.
1885	Juana moves to Mayfield, California, to be near her daughters.
1886	Juana Briones dies.
1997	Memorial to Juana Briones is placed in Washington Square in San Francisco.

Glossary

adobe—sundried bricks made from clay and straw or grass; often a basic building material

aguardiente—a distilled liquor; a grape brandy

alcalde—Spanish title for mayor of a pueblo

Alta California—northern section of California. Baja California is the southern section

la bamba—a Spanish dance

bishop—the title of a priest with a position of authority within the Catholic Church

Californio—Spanish word for a Hispanic California settler during the rancho period

cobbler—a person who makes shoes by hand for a living

comandante—the Spanish word for commander

comisionado—Spanish word for a soldier who was commissioned to do a specific job

curandera—Spanish word for healer or medical person who uses natural forms of healing

dichos—Spanish term for sayings or proverbs

fiesta—Spanish word for party or celebration

indios—Spanish word for Indians

jump ship—to flee from duty on a ship

mass—a Catholic Church service

mis hijos—Spanish expression for "my children"

mission—a religious center that was the home of padres and Christianized Indians

neophytes—Christianized Indians

New Spain—the name for Mexico, including what is now Texas, California, Arizona, and New Mexico, before Mexico won its independence from Spain

padre—Spanish for priest; means father

presidio—a military center or fort

pueblo—a village or town

ramada—a temporary shelter with four corner posts and a roof of leaves, grass, and/or branches for shade

rancho—Spanish word for ranch or land given by the king to Spanish settlers

reata—Spanish word for lasso

secularization—the process by which mission lands were taken from the control of the Catholic church and given to individuals

tule—a reed or bulrush that grows near or in swamps and lakes

vaquero—Spanish word for cowboy

vestments—special clothing worn by the padres for performing religious services

viceroy—the king of Spain's representative in New Spain; the leader of New Spain

Yankee—a general term used by Spanish settlers for all non-Hispanic visitors to early California

Family Tree

Marcos Briones *married* Maria Isadora Tapia

- Luz Briones
- Guadalupe Briones
- Felipe Briones
- Gregorio Briones
- Jachaca Briones

Apolinario Miranda *married* Juana Briones

- Maria Presentación Miranda
- Maria Josefa Manuela Miranda
- Maria Jesus Miranda
- Maria de Jesus Miranda del Refugio Miranda
- Maria Antonia Miranda
- Maria Julian Miranda
- Jose Julian Miranda
- Maria Manuela de Jesus Miranda
- Jose Aniceto Miranda